FORBIDDEN FOODS THE HEALTHY WAY

WITH KATIE BRAMLETT

For information contact; Warrior Media, Inc.
c/o The Warrior Wife
PO Box 1499, Soquel Ca 95073
thewarriorwife.com

Book and Cover design by Andrea Horowitt
Production Director Ben Chargin
Recipe Photos by Bryon Rafetto, Shelby Clemons, Marina Martinez
Editing by CD Johnson
Content Contributor Kaitie Korver

Property of Warrior Media, Inc. ISBN: 9780997770346
First Edition December 2017
10 9 8 7 6 5 4 3 2 1

INTRODUCTION

My Take on Eating Healthy

Things in our culture have become so confusing around knowing what is "healthy" (or not), and I want to make it as simple as possible for you. My personal philosophy is based on the idea that human beings were designed to eat simply. Processed food has made simple eating extremely complex for most of us. And the bottom line is...if it comes in ready-to-eat packaging, it's probably not that great for you.

Humans have been hunters and gathers for centuries, eating basic, whole foods such as meats, fruits, vegetables, tubers, herbs, and so on. For the ms part, we've moved away from this real food model into a complex, processed food, fad-dieting society. So if you're trying to figure out what is healthy, all you have to do is ask, "Is this a real food?" Once you answer this with a resounding YES!, you can go on to more complex questions about things like organic foods, meat quality, and best dairy options. I go over these below.

With all of that said, I want you to know that I'm a big believer in balance. There've been times where I let my need for perfect nutrition cause lots of needless stress. I'm a lot happier when I allow myself to bend the rules once in awhile. And you will be, too! The bottom line is that what you eat needs to make sense for YOU. If you're struggling with a major health challenge, you may be in a place where bending the rules every once in awhile isn't possible until your health improves. Listen to and trust your body; it knows the way.

Why Organic?

I believe in looking at nutrition in the most simple way possible. I ask myself, "How is food supposed to be?" I also ask myself how my body was meant to process food in the first place. When I get the answers to these questions, decisions become simple... and if I have the choice between eating fruit covered in pesticides and one that was grown organically, I'm going with the organic option.

Why I Include Dairy

I've been blessed that my body does great with most dairy. I know this is not the case for others. If your body can't handle dairy, you should avoid it. There are a lot of great alternatives today, like almond or coconut milk. Personally, I avoid soy milk because it's estrogenic.

Why I Buy Full-Fat Dairy Products

When I buy dairy, I get full-fat dairy products. The reason is because full-fat dairy products are less processed. Also, you should know that fat is actually good for you. The only thing you need to remember about this is that not all fats are created equally. I'll provide you with a list of healthy fats and others to avoid.

Why Quality Dairy Products Are a Big Deal

It pays to buy quality dairy products that don't contain unnecessary hormones and other harmful preservatives in them. The highest-quality dairy product you can buy is full-fat, organic, and grassfed. This means that the animals' nutrition came from roaming around on a farm eating grass rather than grains and any, other processed foods. Below is a list of healthy fats.

Healthy Fats

- Animal fats (from good organic sources)
- Olive oil (from good organic sources)
- Coconut oil (from good organic sources)
- Avocado oil (from good organic sources)
- Butter (from organic, grass-fed cows)
- Ghee (from organic, grass-fed cows)
- *smoke points vary

Fats to Avoid

- Any type of seed oil (like sunflower or sesame)
- Hydrogenated oils (like shortening or margarine)
- Any type of "cooking oils" (other than what is listed above)

Selecting Meats

I wish going to the store and buying high-quality, healthy beef was a no-brainer. Unfortunately, our food system is a big business, and mass production is the priority. Most animals are kept in small, confined spaces and they eat a highly processed, grain-based diet. This doesn't produce a high-quality, nutrient-dense meat for us to consume. If you're avoiding processed grains, but eat an animal that lived on such food, you're eating processed grains, too.

The Best Type of Meat to Purchase

- 100% grass-fed or pastured-raised beef or lamb
- Organic, free-range chicken
- Organic, nitrate-free pork
- Wild-caught seafood (farm-raised seafood falls along the same lines as a "processed food")

Canned Foods

Researchers have discovered a laundry list of negative side effects linked to BPA, which can be found in plastics and canned goods. It's healthier if you avoid them. That written, some of the recipes in this book call for canned ingredients. When possible, search for cans labeled "BPA Free."

Let's Get Started

I'm excited for you to try these recipes, and I also want to offer some encouragement. Trying a new recipe may take a little patience. While these are pretty straightforward, it might take a little practice before you feel like you've mastered any of the recipes. Give yourself time, and enjoy the learning process.

TABLE OF CONTENTS

My take on bread...

Did you know that the average bread you buy from the grocery store has gluten in it? And did you also know there are TWO big things wrong with gluten?

- First of all, it's very addictive because it contains a super carbohydrate called Amylopectin A.
- Second of all, gluten contains lectins that are specific to wheat. Lectins are plant proteins that help you stay alive.

I want to share why both Amylopectin A and wheat lectins are so dangerous to your health and why I created an alternative for you.

Amylopectin A is what some people would call a "super starch." It is digested very quickly, and it raises your blood sugar levels very, VERY high.

A 1995 study by the National Institutes of Health found that, over the course of 12 weeks, insulin resistance increased to dangerous levels if Amylopectin A was consumed. Traditionally-made <u>wheat bread isn't the same wheat bread that our ancestors used to eat.</u>

Amylopectin A is the stuff of your diet nightmares.

Wheat germ lectins, on the other hand, damage the lining of our digestive system - and this happens regardless of whether or not you are gluten intolerant.

Have you ever noticed that your bloating goes down when you remove whet from your diet? Well...there's a reason for that, and that reason is because you're no longer consuming lectins.

All the bread recipes that follow are 100% gluten-free, which means that they will not harm the lining of your stomach or intestines.

And they are safe for you and anyone with gluten intolerance or sensitivity.

I hope you enjoy!

BREADS

GLUTEN-FREE BANANA LOAF

Prep Time: 15 minutes | Cook Time: 40-45 minutes | Serves: 12

INGREDIENTS

- Coconut oil Spray, as needed
- ½ cup almond flour
- 1/2 cup coconut flour
- 1 tablespoon tapioca starch
- 1 1/4 teaspoon baking soda
- 1/2 teaspoon salt
- 4 ripe bananas
- 2 tablespoon coconut oil, plus more for greasing your pan
- 1/2 teaspoon vanilla extract
- 4 eggs
- Cacao nibs, toasted pecans or walnuts, optional

DIRECTIONS

1. Preheat the oven to 350° F. Lightly grease a 9x5" loaf pan with coconut oil spray and line with parchment paper.
2. In a bowl, whisk together the dry ingredients. In another bowl, cream together the bananas, coconut oil and vanilla. Once they are fully combined, whisk in the eggs and beat until smooth.
3. Fold the dry ingredients into the wet and stir until fully incorporated. Add in any additions if desired.
4. Pour the batter into the prepared pan and bake for 40-45 minutes until a toothpick comes out clean when inserted into the center. Allow to cool before slicing.

GINGERBREAD LOAF

Prep time: 15 minutes | Cook time: 30-40 minutes | Serves: 12

INGREDIENTS

- Coconut oil spray, as needed
- ⅔ cup molasses
- 4 eggs
- ¼ cup full-fat coconut milk
- 1 teaspoon vanilla extract
- ⅓ cup coconut oil, melted
- ½ cup almond flour
- ½ cup coconut flour
- 1 teaspoon cinnamon
- ½ teaspoon cloves
- 1 teaspoon ginger
- 1 teaspoon nutmeg
- ¼ teaspoon salt
- 1 teaspoon baking soda

DIRECTIONS

1. Preheat the oven to 400° F. Lightly grease a 9x5" loaf pan with coconut oil spray and line with parchment paper.
2. In a small bowl, whisk together the wet ingredients and the dry in another. Fold the wet ingredients into the dry and mix until there are no lumps.
3. Pour the batter into the prepared pan and bake for 30-40 minutes, or until a toothpick comes out clean when inserted in the center. Cool slightly before serving.

RASPBERRY LEMON POPPYSEED BREAD

Prep Time: 15 minutes | Cook Time: 40-50 minutes | Serves: 12

INGREDIENTS

- Coconut oil spray, as needed
- ½ cup zucchini, peeled and grated
- 1½ cups almond meal
- ¼ cup coconut flour
- ¼ cup tapioca starch
- ½ teaspoon baking soda
- ½ teaspoon baking powder
- Pinch of salt
- ⅓ cup coconut oil
- ⅓ cup honey
- 2 teaspoon lemon extract
- 3 eggs, whisked
- ½ cup raspberries
- 1-2 tablespoon poppy seeds

For the sauce:
- 1 cup raspberries
- 2 tablespoon lemon juice
- 2 tablespoon honey
- 2 tablespoon water

DIRECTIONS

1. Preheat the oven to 350° F. Lightly grease a 9x5" loaf pan with coconut oil spray and line with parchment paper. Peel and shred the zucchini, then squeeze out the excess moisture with a clean dish towel. Place in a colander and set aside.
2. In a large bowl, whisk together the dry ingredients. In another bowl, whisk together the wet ingredients and whisk until smooth. Stir the wet ingredients into the dry, along with the zucchini, poppy seeds and raspberries. Stir until fully incorporated.
3. Pour the batter into the prepared pan and bake for about 45-50 minutes, or until a toothpick comes out clean when inserted in the center.
4. For the sauce, combine all the ingredients and simmer for 10-12 minutes. Puree and strain, then drizzle over the top of the cooled bread before slicing and serving.

GLUTEN-FREE CHOCOLATE ZUCCHINI BREAD

Prep time: 15 minutes | Cook time: 30-45 minutes | Serves: 12

INGREDIENTS

- Coconut oil spray, as needed
- 1½ cups zucchini, shredded
- 2 eggs, whisked
- ¾ cup cashew butter
- ⅓ cup coconut sugar
- ¼ cup cocoa powder
- 2 tablespoons almond flour
- 1 teaspoon vanilla extract
- ½ teaspoon baking powder
- ½ teaspoon baking soda
- Pinch of salt

DIRECTIONS

1. Preheat the oven to 375° F. Lightly grease a 9x5" loaf pan with coconut oil spray and line with parchment paper. Peel and shred the zucchini, then squeeze out the excess moisture with a clean dish towel. Place in a colander and set aside.

2. Combine all the wet ingredients in a large bowl and combine all the dry ingredients in a small bowl. Whisk the wet ingredients until incorporated, then fold in the dry ingredients.

3. Fold in the zucchini, then pour the batter into the prepared pan and bake for about 30-40 minutes or until a toothpick comes out clean when inserted in the center. Cool slightly before serving.

GLUTEN-FREE BREAD

Prep time: 15 minutes | Cook time: 45-60 minutes | Serves: 12

INGREDIENTS

- Coconut oil spray, as needed
- 1½ cups almond flour
- 3 tablespoon coconut flour
- ¼ cup flax meal
- ¼ teaspoon salt
- 1½ teaspoon baking soda
- 5 eggs, whisked
- ¼ cup coconut oil
- 1 tablespoon honey
- 1 tablespoon apple cider vinegar

DIRECTIONS

1. Preheat the oven to 350° F. Lightly grease a 9x5" loaf pan with coconut oil spray and line with parchment paper.
2. In a food processor, place the almond flour, coconut flour, flax meal, salt and baking soda.
3. With the machine running, slowly add the eggs one at a time, then the coconut oil, honey and vinegar. Pulse just until the batter comes together.
4. Pour the batter into the prepared pan and bake for about 45-50 minutes or until a toothpick comes out clean when inserted in the center. Cool slightly before slicing.

GLUTEN-FREE BUTTERMILK LOAF

Prep time: 15 minutes | Cook time: 35-40 minutes | Serves: 12

INGREDIENTS

- Coconut oil spray, as needed
- 2 cups almond flour
- ½ cup coconut flour
- ¼ teaspoon salt
- 1 teaspoon baking soda
- 4 eggs
- ⅔ cup honey
- ⅔ cup coconut oil
- ¾ cup canned coconut milk
- 2 tablespoons vanilla extract

DIRECTIONS

1. Preheat the oven to 350° F. Lightly grease a 9x5" inch loaf pan with coconut oil spray and line with parchment paper.
2. In a bowl, combine the almond flour, coconut flour, salt, and baking soda and in a separate bowl, combine the wet ingredients.
3. Mix the wet into the dry and stir until there are no lumps. Pour the batter into the prepared pan and bake for 35-40 minutes, or until a toothpick inserted in the center comes out clean. Cool slightly before slicing.

GLUTEN-FREE CHERRY ALMOND BREAD

Prep time: 15 minutes | Cook time: 50-60 minutes | Serves: 12

INGREDIENTS

- Coconut oil spray, as needed
- 3 cups almond flour
- ¼ cup coconut flour
- 6 tablespoon tapioca starch
- ½ teaspoon baking soda
- 1 ½ teaspoon baking powder
- ½ cup coconut sugar
- ½ teaspoon salt
- 5 tablespoon coconut oil, melted
- ⅓ cup canned coconut milk
- 3 eggs
- 2-3 teaspoon almond extract
- 4 ounce dried cherries, roughly chopped (no sugar added)
- ½-1 cup slivered almonds

DIRECTIONS

1. Preheat the oven to 350° F. Lightly grease a 9x5" loaf pan with coconut oil spray and line with parchment paper.
2. In a large bowl, combine all the dry ingredients. In another bowl, combine the wet ingredients and stir to incorporate. Pour the wet into the dry and whisk well, then fold in the cherries and almonds.
3. Pour the batter into the prepared pan and bake for about a 50-60 minutes, or until a toothpick comes out clean when inserted in the center. If the top starts to get too dark, lightly tent with foil and continue to bake until done in the center. Cool slightly before slicing.

GLUTEN-FREE CRANBERRY ORANGE BREAD

Prep time: 15 minutes | Cook time: 45-60 minutes | Serves: 12

INGREDIENTS

- Coconut oil spray, as needed
- 6 eggs
- 1 orange, zested and juiced (about 2 tablespoon zest and ¼ cup juice)
- ¾ cup canned coconut milk
- ⅓ cup honey
- 2 tablespoon coconut oil
- 1 teaspoon vanilla extract
- ⅔ cup coconut flour
- 1 teaspoon baking soda
- ¼ teaspoon salt
- 1½ cups frozen cranberries

For the glaze:
- 2 tablespoons coconut oil, melted
- 2 tablespoons honey
- 1 tablespoon full-fat coconut milk
- 1 tablespoon orange zest (use some orange juice to thin it out if necessary)

DIRECTIONS

1. Preheat the oven to 350° F. Lightly grease a 9x5" loaf pan with coconut oil spray and line with parchment paper.
2. Combine the dry ingredients in a bowl and the wet ingredients in another. Whisk the dry ingredients into the wet and stir until fully incorporated. Fold in the cranberries and pour the batter into the prepared pan.
3. Bake for about 45-50 minutes or until a toothpick comes out clean when inserted in the center.
4. To make the glaze, whisk all ingredients together until smooth. Once the loaf has cooled, drizzle over the top, then slice and serve.

GLUTEN-FREE CARROT BREAD

Prep time: 15 minutes | Cook time: 45-60 minutes | Serves: 12

INGREDIENTS

- Coconut oil spray, as needed
- ⅔ cup honey
- ⅓ cup coconut oil, melted
- 2 tablespoon almond butter (or nut butter of choice)
- 2 eggs
- 1 cup almond flour
- ¼ cup tapioca flour
- 1 tablespoon coconut flour
- ½ teaspoon salt
- 1 teaspoon vanilla extract
- ½ teaspoon baking soda
- ½ teaspoon baking powder
- 1 teaspoon cinnamon
- ½ teaspoon nutmeg
- 1 cup carrots, shredded
- ½ cup pecans or walnuts (or nut of choice), chopped
- ⅓ cup raisins

DIRECTIONS

1. Preheat the oven to 350° F. Lightly grease a 9x5" loaf pan with coconut oil spray and line with parchment paper.
2. In a large bowl, combine the honey, coconut oil and nut butter. Whisk in the eggs and stir until well incorporated.
3. In another bowl, whisk together the dry ingredients. Fold the dry into the wet ingredients and mix well, then fold in the carrots, nuts and raisins.
4. Pour the batter into the prepared pan and bake for about 40-50 minutes or until a toothpick comes out clean when inserted into the center. Cool slightly before slicing.

GLUTEN-FREE ZUCCHINI BREAD

Prep time: 15 minutes | Cook time: 40-50 minutes | Serves: 12

INGREDIENTS

- Coconut oil spray, as needed
- 6 eggs
- ½ cup maple syrup
- ¼ cup coconut oil, melted
- 1 teaspoon vanilla extract
- ¾ cup coconut flour
- 1 teaspoon cinnamon
- ¼ teaspoon nutmeg
- 1 teaspoon salt
- ¾ teaspoon baking soda
- 1½ cups zucchini, shredded and tightly packed
- 1 cup walnuts (or nut of choice), chopped

DIRECTIONS

1. Preheat the oven to 350° F. Lightly grease a 9x5" loaf pan with coconut oil spray and line with parchment paper. Peel and shred the zucchini, then squeeze out the excess moisture with a clean dish towel. Place in a colander and set aside.

2. In a large bowl, whisk together the eggs, maple syrup, coconut oil and vanilla until smooth. In another bowl, combine the dry ingredients. Fold the dry ingredients into the wet and stir until everything is incorporated and no lumps remain.

3. Fold in the zucchini and nuts, then pour the batter into the prepared pan. Bake for about 45-50 minutes, or until a toothpick comes out clean when inserted in the center. Cool slightly before slicing.

GLUTEN-FREE "CORNBREAD"

Prep time: 15 minutes | Cook time: 40-45 minutes | Serves: 12

INGREDIENTS

- Coconut oil spray, as needed
- 2 tablespoons apple cider vinegar
- 2 tablespoons coconut sugar or honey
- 1 cup water
- ¼ cup coconut oil, melted
- 4 eggs
- 10 tablespoons coconut flour
- ¼ teaspoon salt
- ½ teaspoon baking soda

DIRECTIONS

1. Preheat the oven to 350° F. Lightly grease an 8x8" baking dish with coconut oil spray and line with parchment paper (a muffin pan with liners works well too).
2. In a blender or food processor, combine the apple cider vinegar, coconut sugar, water and coconut oil. Process until smooth, then add the eggs one at a time while the machine is running. Blend until smooth after each addition.
3. Add the coconut flour, salt and baking soda and blend. Pour into the prepared pan and bake for about 40-45 minutes or until a toothpick comes out clean when inserted in the center. If making muffins, the bake time will be less.

GLUTEN-FREE CINNAMON APPLE BREAD

Prep time: 15 minutes | Cook time: 50-60 minutes | Serves: 12

INGREDIENTS

- 2 cups creamy almond butter (or nut butter of your choice)
- ½ teaspoon salt
- 1 tablespoon cinnamon
- 4 eggs
- ½ cup honey or maple syrup
- 1 tablespoon vanilla extract
- 1 teaspoon baking soda
- 2 teaspoon apple cider vinegar
- 1 cup pecans (or nut of choice), chopped
- 2 cups apples, shredded or diced

DIRECTIONS

1. Preheat the oven to 350° F. Lightly grease a 9x5" loaf pan with coconut oil spray and line with parchment paper.
2. In a large bowl, combine the nut butter, salt, cinnamon, eggs and honey or maple syrup and vanilla. Stir until fully incorporated.
3. Sprinkle the baking soda on the top of the batter, then pour the vinegar on top. The mixture will foam a little, then fold it all together. Fold in the nuts and apples, then pour the batter into the prepared pan and bake for about 50-60 minutes or until a toothpick comes out clean when inserted in the center. Cool slightly before slicing.

My take on adult beverages...

DISCLAIMER: I know we all know this, but I feel like I have to say it anyway. If you have any troubles with addiction, you probably want to avoid alcohol entirely or seriously limit your use of it. Now this is a no-judgement zone when it comes to drinking, and I want to share a little bit about my way of preparing adult beverages so that you can be your healthiest at all times.

Now, most adults I know have at least one alcoholic drink each week. This wouldn't be a big deal, except for the way that alcohol affects your body.

I'll never forget the day I learned exactly why alcohol contributes so much to weight gain. Looking back, it made a lot of sense.

See, alcohol is naturally a neurotoxin. What that means is that it is toxic to your central nervous system.

When alcohol enters your bloodstream, all your body wants to do is get rid of it. As a matter of fact, your metabolism stops working normally until it has processed all the alcohol from your system.

Even knowing that little bit, I still drank occasionally. So, what I decided to do was to find ways I could both cut the calories in adult beverages and also make them healthier in any way possible.

In the drink recipes you'll find on the next pages, you'll see fresh juice or fresh fruit substituted for the chemical-laden coloring and flavoring you'll traditionally find in these drinks.

You'll also find alternatives to refined sugar and traditional soft drinks. Additionally, all the drinks use gluten-free alcohol.

They are tasty and refreshing, and I hope you like them as much as my friends, family, and I have!

DRINKS

SPIKED LEMONADE

Prep time: 10 minutes | Serves: 1

INGREDIENTS

- 1 lemon, juiced
- 1½ oz. gluten-free lemon or regular vodka
- 1 cup sparkling water
- Honey or liquid stevia, to taste
- Lemon slices, for garnish

DIRECTIONS

1. Combine all ingredients and pour over ice.

GRAPEFRUIT MOJITO

Prep time: 10 minutes | Serves: 1

INGREDIENTS

- Honey or liquid stevia, to taste
- 2-4 oz. grapefruit juice (or 1 whole grapefruit, juiced)
- Fresh mint, to taste
- 1½ oz. gluten-free vodka
- Sparkling water
- Sliced grapefruit, for serving

DIRECTIONS

1. In a shaker, place the honey or stevia, grapefruit juice and mint and muddle well. Add the vodka and shake well, the pour over a glass full of ice. Top off with sparkling water.

MOSCOW MULE

Prep time: 10 minutes | Serves: 1

INGREDIENTS

- 2 oz. gluten-free vodka
- 1 oz. lime juice
- Stevia sweetened ginger ale or ginger beer (Zevia is a good brand)
- Ice, as needed
- Lime wedges, for garnish

DIRECTIONS

1. Fill a glass with ice cubes. Add the gluten-free vodka and lime juice and top with ginger beer. Garnish with a lime slice.

COCONUT COOLER

Prep time: 10 minutes | Serves: 1

INGREDIENTS

- 2 oz. gluten-free vodka
- 2-4 oz. coconut water
- Squeeze of lime juice, if desired
- Ice, as needed

DIRECTIONS

1. Mix the gluten-free vodka and coconut water and pour over ice. Serve with a squeeze of lime juice, if desired.

FRUIT EXPLOSION

Prep time: 10 minutes | Serves: 1

INGREDIENTS

- ½ orange, juiced
- ½ cup peach
- ½ cup strawberries
- 4 raspberries
- 8 blueberries
- ½ cup crushed ice
- 1½ oz. tequila
- 4 oz. sparkling water

DIRECTIONS

1. Muddle the strawberries, peach, blueberries and raspberries, then vigorously shake with the rest of the ingredients except for the sparkling water. Strain into a glass and top with sparkling water.

BLOODY MARY

Prep time: 10 minutes | Serves: 1

INGREDIENTS

- ¾ cup tomato juice
- ½ lemon, juiced
- Dash of hot sauce
- Dash of gluten free Worcestershire
- Freshly ground pepper, to taste
- 1½ oz. gluten-free vodka
- Lemon wedges, for garnish
- Celery sticks, for garnish

DIRECTIONS

1. Combine the tomato juice, lemon juice, hot sauce, Worcestershire, pepper and gluten-free vodka and serve with a lemon wedge and celery stick.

NORCAL MARGARITA

Prep time: 10 minutes | Serves: 1

INGREDIENTS

- 2-3 oz. tequila
- 1 lime, juiced
- ½ orange, juiced
- Sparkling water, as needed
- Lime wedges, for garnish
- Ice, as needed

DIRECTIONS

1. Shake the tequila, lime and orange juice with ice, then strain into a glass with ice and top off with sparkling water. Garnish with a slice of lime, if desired.

MOJITO

Prep time: 10 minutes | Serves: 1

INGREDIENTS

- 10-12 mint leaves
- ½ lime, juiced
- Liquid stevia, to taste or honey (dissolve in 1-2 tablespoons of water)
- 1½ oz. gluten-free vodka
- Sparkling water, as needed
- Lime wedges, for garnish
- Ice, as needed

DIRECTIONS

1. In the bottom of a glass, muddle the mint leaves with the lime juice and honey syrup, or stevia if using. Add ice, and then shake with gluten-free vodka. Top with sparkling water and garnish with a lime wedge, if desired.

PIÑA COLADA

Prep time: 10 minutes | Serves: 1

INGREDIENTS

- 2 oz. gluten-free vodka
- 3-4 oz. 100% pineapple juice
- 3-4 oz. full-fat coconut milk
- Liquid stevia, to taste
- Ice, as needed
- Fresh pineapple, optional for serving

DIRECTIONS

1. Combine all ingredients in a blender and puree until smooth. Serve with a wedge of fresh pineapple.

CUCUMBER LIME COOLER

Prep time: 10 minutes | Serves: 2

INGREDIENTS

- 1½ oz. gluten-free vodka
- ¼ cup cucumber juice
- ½ lime, juiced
- Liquid stevia, to taste
- Handful fresh mint leaves
- Ice, as needed

DIRECTIONS

1. Shake all ingredients well in a cocktail shaker, then strain into a glass with ice.

WATERMELON MOJITO

Prep time: 10 minutes | Serves: 1

INGREDIENTS

- ½ cup watermelon
- ½ lime, juiced
- 1½ oz. tequila
- 2 fresh mint leaves
- 1 cup crushed ice
- 4 oz. sparkling water

DIRECTIONS

1. Muddle the watermelon, then shake vigorously with the tequila, mint leaves and ice. Strain into a glass and top with sparkling water.

PINEAPPLE DROP

Prep time: 10 minutes | Serves: 1

INGREDIENTS

- ½ cup pineapple
- ½ orange, juiced
- ½ lemon, juiced
- Crushed ice, as needed
- 1½ oz. gluten-free vodka
- 4 oz. lemon sparkling water

DIRECTIONS

1. Muddle the pineapple, then vigorously shake with all the ingredients except for the sparkling water. Strain into a glass and top with lemon sparkling water.

KATIE COSMO

Prep time: 10 minutes | Serves: 1

INGREDIENTS

- 1 cup ice
- 1½ oz. gluten-free vodka
- 1 lime, juiced
- 2 oz. 100% cranberry juice
- 4 oz. lime sparkling water

DIRECTIONS

1. Vigorously shake all ingredients except for the sparkling water in a cocktail shaker. Strain into a glass and top with lime sparkling water.

KOMBUCHA MARGARITA

Prep time: 10 minutes | Serves: 2

INGREDIENTS

- 3 oz. tequila
- 1 orange, juiced
- 3 limes, juiced
- Liquid stevia, to taste
- 6 oz. kombucha
- Salt, for the rim
- Ice, as needed

DIRECTIONS

1. Run a lime wedge along the rim of the glasses and dip it in the salt. Shake all the ingredients except for the kombucha with ice. Add the kombucha and strain into salt-rimmed glasses.

BLACKBERRY MINT MOJITO

Prep time: 10 minutes | Serves: 1

INGREDIENTS

- 3 blackberries
- ½ lime, juiced
- ½ lemon, juiced
- 1½ oz. gluten-free vodka
- 4 oz. sparkling water, as needed
- Ice, as needed
- 3 fresh mint leaves

DIRECTIONS

1. Muddle the blackberries and the mint, then add the vodka and ice and shake vigorously. Strain into a glass with ice and top off with sparkling water.

BLUEBERRY BLISS

Prep time: 10 minutes | Serves: 1

INGREDIENTS

- ½ cup watermelon
- ½ lime, juiced
- 1½ oz. tequila
- 2 fresh mint leaves
- 1 cup crushed ice
- 4 oz. sparkling water

DIRECTIONS

1. Muddle the watermelon, then shake vigorously with the tequila, mint leaves and ice. Strain into a glass and top with sparkling water.

STRAWBERRY PEACH PARADISE

Prep time: 10 minutes | Serves: 1

INGREDIENTS

- ½ cup strawberries
- ½ cup peach
- 1½ oz. gluten-free vodka
- ½ lime, juiced
- ½ cup crushed ice
- 4 oz. lemon sparkling water

DIRECTIONS

1. Muddle the strawberries and the peach, then vigorously shake with the rest of the ingredients except for the sparkling water. Strain into a glass and top with lemon sparkling water.

RASPBERRY CITRUS SPARKLER

Prep time: 10 minutes | Serves: 1

INGREDIENTS

- ½ cup raspberries
- ½ cup pineapple
- ½ lime, juiced
- ½ lemon, juiced
- 1 cup crushed ice
- 6 oz. lemon sparkling water

DIRECTIONS

1. Muddle the raspberries and pineapple, then vigorously shake with the other ingredients except for the sparkling water. Strain into a glass and top with the lemon sparkling water.

PARADISE MINT FUSION

Prep time: 10 minutes | Serves: 1

INGREDIENTS

- ½ orange, juiced
- 2 oz. 100% cranberry juice
- 6 fresh mint leaves
- 1 cup crushed ice
- 1½ oz. tequila
- ½ lime, juiced
- 4 oz. lime sparkling water

DIRECTIONS

1. Vigorously shake all ingredients except for the sparkling water. Strain into a glass and top with lime sparkling water.

TROPICAL SPARKLER

Prep time: 10 minutes | Serves: 1

INGREDIENTS

- ½ cup watermelon
- ½ cup pineapple
- ½ cup crushed ice
- ½ lemon, juiced
- 1½ oz. gluten-free vodka
- 4 oz. lemon sparkling water

DIRECTIONS

1. Muddle the watermelon and pineapple. Shake vigorously with the rest of the ingredients except for the sparkling water. Strain into a glass and top with lemon sparkling water.

STRAWBERRY MOJITO

Prep time: 10 minutes | Serves: 1

INGREDIENTS

- ½ cup strawberries
- 8 fresh mint leaves
- ½ lime, juiced
- ½ cup crushed ice
- 1½ oz. tequila
- 4 oz. lime sparkling water

DIRECTIONS

1. Muddle the strawberries and the mint, then vigorously shake with the rest of the ingredients except for the sparkling water. Strain into a glass and top with lime sparkling water.

My take on sweet treats...

Even if you don't have a raging sweet tooth like me, almost everyone enjoys sweets every now and then.

Whether it's after dinner for dessert, on long trips when you want a sugary snack for a tiny jolt of energy, or late at night just before you go to bed, sweets are a food group for many of us.

The problem is that most sweet treats you buy from the grocery store are filled with all sorts of chemicals you can't pronounce. And on top of that, the sugar levels are out of this world.

If you love sweets, you'll eventually need a huge amount of self control or you'll have to find a better way to eat them.

What I decided to do was make my sweet treats at home and use whole food ingredients instead of anything processed.

And I really don't rely on refined sugar, either! It's made a huge difference.

The treats on the following pages are all gluten-free, and they are as nutritious as they are yummy.

You still don't want to overdo it when eating sweet treats made the Warrior Wife Way, but I won't blame you if you do!

SWEET TREATS

SWEETENED WHIPPED CREAM WITH FRESH STRAWBERRIES

Prep Time: 15 min | Serves: 4

INGREDIENTS

- 1 cup heavy cream
- 1 tablespoon vanilla
- A few drops of sweetener, maple syrup, honey, liquid stevia
- 2 pints sliced fresh strawberries, or berry of choice

DIRECTIONS

1. Pour chilled heavy cream into a bowl and whip until thick and fluffy, using a whisk, hand or stand mixer. Add the vanilla and sweetener.
2. Serve with the berries and a square of dark chocolate, if desired.

CHOCOLATE DIPPED BANANA BITES

Prep time: 2 hours | Serves: 3

INGREDIENTS

- 3 large bananas
- ⅓ cup nut butter of choice
- ½ cup melted dark chocolate

DIRECTIONS

1. Slice bananas into slices about ¼-½ inch thick.
2. Spread a little nut butter onto a banana and sandwich two slices together.
3. Place on parchment paper on a baking sheet and freeze until solid, about an hour.
4. Melt chocolate and remove frozen banana bites from freezer.
5. Quickly dip each banana bite in chocolate and place back on wax paper. Freeze for another hour before serving.
6. Store in an airtight container in the freezer for up to 2 weeks

CINNAMON TOASTED ALMONDS WITH BERRIES

Prep time: 15 minutes | Cook time: 5-10 minutes | Serves: 2

INGREDIENTS

- 2 tablespoons slivered almonds
- ½ teaspoon cinnamon
- 1 bag frozen mixed berries
- ¼ cup unsweetened coconut flakes

DIRECTIONS

1. Preheat the oven to 325° F and place almonds on a parchment lined baking sheet. Sprinkle with cinnamon. Bake for 5-10 minutes until golden brown. They brown quickly so keep an eye on them.
2. In a small pot, dump your berries in and cook them on low heat until they start to break down. You want it to be a chunky texture, not too runny.
3. Place the berries in a bowl and sprinkle with the cinnamon almonds and coconut flakes.

VANILLA CHIA PUDDING

Prep time: 3 hours | Serves: 4

INGREDIENTS

- ½ cup chia seeds
- 1 vanilla bean, split and seeds scraped
- 1 cup cashews, soaked in filtered water for 2 hours to overnight
- 4 cups filtered water
- 8 Medjool dates, pitted
- Pinch of salt
- ¼ teaspoon cinnamon
- 2 tablespoons coconut butter
- 4 teaspoon vanilla extract
- 2 cups mixed raspberries and blueberries, for serving

DIRECTIONS

1. Place chia seeds in a medium mixing bowl, and set aside.
2. Drain cashews, and rinse well. Add cashews, filtered water, dates, salt, cinnamon, coconut butter, vanilla extract, and vanilla seeds to a blender. Blend on high speed for 2 minutes, and pour into bowl with chia seeds. Whisk well. Let mixture sit for 10 to 15 minutes, whisking every few minutes to prevent chia seeds from clumping (pudding will thicken quickly). Refrigerate until cold, about 3 hours.
3. Whisk pudding before serving and top with berries.

KEY LIME PIE

Prep time: 60 minutes | Serves: 8-12

INGREDIENTS

Crust:
- 1½ cups almond flour
- ¼ cup coconut oil
- 2 tablespoons honey

Filling:
- 2 avocados
- 1 cup dates, pitted and softened in hot water
- ¼ coconut butter, softened
- ⅓-½ cup key lime juice (or regular lime juice)
- 1 tablespoon lime zest
- 1 teaspoon vanilla

DIRECTIONS

1. In a bowl, mix together the almond flour, melted coconut oil and honey until it comes together as a dough.
2. Press the dough into a pie pan, then place in a freezer while making the filling.
3. In a blender or food processor, process the avocados, dates (drained), coconut butter, lime juice, zest, and vanilla until smooth.
4. Pour the filling into pie crust and place in the refrigerator for about one hour to set up before slicing and serving.

ALMOND BUTTER BROWNIES

Prep time: 10 minutes | Cook time: 30-45 minutes | Serves: 8

INGREDIENTS

- 1 (16 oz.) jar creamy roasted almond butter
- 2 eggs
- 1¼ cups honey
- 1 tablespoon vanilla extract
- ½ cup unsweetened cocoa powder
- ½ teaspoon salt
- 1 teaspoon baking soda
- 1 cup dark chocolate chips (least sugar possible)

DIRECTIONS

1. 1. Preheat oven to 325° F. Lightly grease a 9x13" baking dish with coconut oil and line with parchment paper.
2. In a large bowl, combine the almond butter with the eggs, honey and vanilla until smooth
3. Stir in the cocoa powder, salt and baking soda, then fold in the chocolate chips. Pour the batter in the prepared pan and bake for 35-40 minutes or until a toothpick comes out clean when inserted in the center.

CHOCOLATE CHIP COOKIES

Prep time: 15 minutes | Cook time: 10-15 minutes | Serves: 8

INGREDIENTS

- ¼ cup butter
- ⅓ cup honey
- 1 egg
- 1 tablespoon vanilla extract
- 1 ⅔ cups almond flour
- 1 tablespoon coconut flour
- ½ teaspoon baking soda
- ½ teaspoon salt
- ½ cup dark chocolate chips (least sugar possible)

DIRECTIONS

1. Preheat oven to 350° F.
2. By hand or in a food processor, cream the butter, honey, egg, and vanilla until smooth and fluffy. Add the almond flour, coconut flour, baking soda and salt and mix until everything is incorporated. Stir in the chocolate chips.
3. Scoop dough out into 1½" balls and place on a parchment lined baking sheet. Press each ball of dough down slightly until they are about ½" thick. Bake for 9-12 minutes or until slightly golden around the edges.

FRUIT CRISP

Prep time: 15 minutes | Cook time: 30-40 minutes | Serves: 4

INGREDIENTS

Topping:
- ⅓ cup + 2 teaspoon coconut flour
- 1 cup walnuts, ground
- ¼ cup + 2 tablespoons coconut sugar
- 2 teaspoon vanilla extract, divided
- ½ teaspoon cinnamon
- ¼ cup coconut oil
- ½ cup coconut chips, toasted*

Filling:
- 3 peaches, washed and sliced
- 1 cup blackberries
- 1 cup blueberries
- Juice of one lemon
- Zest of half a lemon
- 2 tablespoons unsalted butter or coconut oil
- ½ teaspoon cinnamon

*Toast coconut chips for 5 minutes at 350° F. Keep an eye on them, they burn fast.

DIRECTIONS

1. Preheat the oven to 350° F. In a medium sized bowl, mix flour with ground walnuts, coconut sugar, 1 teaspoon vanilla extract, cinnamon, coconut oil and coconut chips. Set aside.

2. In a large bowl, mix the fruit with the remaining sugar and vanilla. Pour in the lemon juice and zest and let the fruit sit for about half an hour. Drain the fruit, reserving the liquid. Place the liquid in a pot and add the butter or coconut oil. Set the pot on medium heat and allow the butter/coconut oil to liquefy. Whisk in the 2 teaspoons of coconut flour and allow to simmer for 5 minutes. Mix the liquid back into the fruit.

3. Pour the fruit mixture into a 8x8" baking dish or pie pan. Top with the crumble and bake for 30-35 minutes until top is golden brown.

VANILLA COCONUT MILK ICE CREAM

Prep time: 2 hours | Cook time: 10 minutes | Serves: 4

INGREDIENTS

- 28 ounces full-fat coconut milk
- 1 teaspoon vanilla extract
- ½ cup honey
- 3 egg yolks

DIRECTIONS

1. Slice the vanilla bean lengthwise and scrape out the seeds.
2. In a saucepan, whisk together the coconut milk, vanilla extract, honey and egg yolks. Heat the mixture over medium heat stirring constantly until the mixture coats the back of a spoon, about 8-10 minutes. Don't let it boil.
   Transfer ice cream mixture to a bowl, and cover with plastic wrap.
3. Place the plastic wrap directly on the liquid, so no condensation forms. Place in the refrigerator and chill until cold, at least 2 hours.
4. Using your ice cream maker according to the manufacturer's instructions, process the chilled ice cream mixture. If you don't have an ice cream maker, just place the bowl in the freezer and give it a stir every 15 minutes or so until it's the consistency of ice cream.

CHOCOLATE MOUSSE

Prep time: 10 minutes | Serves: 2

INGREDIENTS

- 1 ripe avocado
- 2–3 tablespoons unsweetened cocoa powder
- ¼ cup full-fat coconut milk
- Liquid stevia, to taste
- ½ teaspoon vanilla extract

DIRECTIONS

1. Scoop out avocado and combine it with the cocoa powder, coconut milk, vanilla and stevia in a food processor.
2. If the mixture is too thick, add a little more coconut milk to thin it out.
   For best results, refrigerate until chilled.

SNICKERDOODLES

Prep time: 15 minutes | Cook time: 25-30 minutes | Serves: 6-8

INGREDIENTS

- 2 cups almond flour
- 2 tablespoons coconut flour
- ¼ cup unsalted butter
- 1 egg
- 1 teaspoon vanilla extract
- ¼ teaspoon baking soda
- ¼ teaspoon salt
- ½ cup honey (you may have to add more coconut flour)*
- 2 tablespoons cinnamon
- Pinch of salt

DIRECTIONS

1. Preheat oven to 350° F and line a baking sheet with parchment paper. In a medium bowl combine almond flour, coconut flour, salt and baking soda until well combined.
2. In a small bowl add egg, vanilla extract, butter, and honey and whisk together. Pour the wet ingredients into dry and mix until thoroughly incorporated and combined. Roll dough into equal sized balls (about one inch in diameter and place them on the baking sheet).
3. In a small bowl, place 2 tablespoons of cinnamon and roll each ball around in the cinnamon until completely coated and place back on the baking sheet evenly spaced apart with enough room for flattening them.
4. Using a cup, flatten each cookie about to about ½" thickness.
5. Bake for 15-20 minutes or until the center of the cookies are no longer completely soft and have a slight resistance to the touch.
6. Place on a wire rack and allow to cool for at least 15 minutes.

*You might need to add more coconut flour to have the dough thick enough to roll into balls. Just make it normally and if you need more, add it by the tablespoon and incorporate it thoroughly until you can roll the dough into balls.

ALMOND BUTTER BLONDIES

Prep time: 15 minutes | Cook time: 30 minutes | Serves: 4-6

INGREDIENTS

- 1 cup almond butter
- ½ cup honey
- 1 egg
- 1 teaspoon vanilla extract
- ½ teaspoon baking soda
  pinch of salt
- ½ cup dark chocolate chips (least sugar possible)

DIRECTIONS

1. Preheat oven to 350° F.
2. Grease an 8x8" baking dish. Mix all ingredients together and fold in chocolate chips.
3. Spread out evenly into baking dish and bake for 20-25 minutes (the top will seem a bit soft but will harden when cooled). Let cool for about 10 minutes before slicing.

MIXED FRUIT AND NUT CLUSTERS

Prep time: 15 minutes | Cook time: 30-40 minutes | Serves: 8-10

INGREDIENTS

- 2 cups dark chocolate chips, (least sugar possible)
- 1½ cup roasted nuts or your choice (cashews, pecans, almonds, walnuts, etc.)
- 1 cup dried fruit of your choice (no sugar added)
- ¼ cup unsweetened shredded coconut
- Pinch of salt

DIRECTIONS

1. Melt chocolate in a bowl.
2. Fold in nuts and fruit.
3. Line a baking pan with parchment paper. Use a spoon to scoop a spoonful of the chocolate mixture and push onto the parchment paper.
4. Sprinkle with a tiny bit of salt and sprinkle with coconut.
5. Place in freezer and let cool for about 30 minutes or more. Once the chocolate is hard, store in the refrigerator in an airtight container.

NO BAKE PEANUT BUTTER PIE

Prep time: 4-6 hours | Serves: 8-10

INGREDIENTS

Crust:
- 1½ cups almond flour
- ¼ cup cocoa powder, unsweetened
- 3-4 tablespoons coconut oil
- Pinch of salt

Filling:
- 1 cup creamy peanut butter, or nut butter of your choice
- ¾ cup water
- ½ cup coconut oil, melted
- ½ cup honey
- Salt, to taste

Chocolate Topping:
- 2 tablespoons coconut oil or unsalted butter, melted
- 2 tablespoons honey
- 3 tablespoons cocoa powder, unsweetened

DIRECTIONS

1. Line an 8" spring-form pan or pie dish with parchment paper. For the crust, combine all of the ingredients in a large mixing bowl and stir well to create a dough. Press the dough evenly into the bottom of the lined pan.
2. For the filling, combine the first four filling ingredients in a blender and process until smooth. Scrape the sides to get the batter very smooth and evenly mixed.
3. Pour the filling onto the crust and smooth the top. Place the pie in the freezer to set until firm, about 4-6 hours.
4. For the chocolate topping, combine the coconut oil, honey and cocoa powder in a bowl. (If your ingredients are cold, this mixture will be clumpy, but it will smooth out when warmed.) Once the pie is completely frozen, drizzle the chocolate over the top.
5. Allow the pie to sit at room temperature for about 15 minutes, to make it easier to slice and serve. Store any remaining pie in the refrigerator for up to one week.

RASPBERRY ALMOND BARS

Prep time: 15 minutes | Cook time: 30-40 minutes | Serves: 8-10

INGREDIENTS

Crust:
- 2 cups almond flour
- 2 tablespoons coconut oil
- 1 tablespoon vanilla extract
- 1 tablespoon water
- ¼ teaspoon salt

Filling:
- 10 ounces frozen raspberries
- ½ cup honey
- 1 teaspoon vanilla extract

Crumb Topping:
- 1 cup walnuts
- ½ cup shredded coconut
- 2 tablespoons honey
- 1 tablespoon coconut oil
- ¼ teaspoon salt

DIRECTIONS

1. Prepare the raspberry filling by heating the ½ cup honey in a medium sized saucepan over medium heat. Bring to a boil, then reduce the heat, add the raspberries and vanilla and simmer for 5 minutes. Cook for 15 minutes, or until thick and place in the refrigerator.
2. For the crust, preheat the oven to 350° F and line an 8x8" baking dish with parchment. Combine all of the crust ingredients in a food processor, and process until the dough comes together in a ball. Press the dough into the bottom of the baking sheet and bake for about 12 minutes. Remove from the oven and allow to cool.
3. For the topping, combine the walnuts, coconut, honey, coconut oil and salt in a food processor, and process until sticky and crumbly, but still coarse in texture.
4. Spread the raspberry filling over the crust, then sprinkle the topping over the raspberry layer. Place back in the oven for 15 minutes or until the topping is golden brown. Allow to cool completely before cutting and serving.

PUMPKIN BARS

Prep time: 20 minutes | Cook time: 30-40 minutes | Serves: 8-10

INGREDIENTS

Crust:
- ½ cup pumpkin puree (no sugar added)
- ½ cup almond butter
- ⅓ cup honey
- 2 eggs
- 2 teaspoon pumpkin pie spice
- 1 teaspoon vanilla extract
- ¼ teaspoon salt
- ½ teaspoon baking soda

Glaze (optional):
- ¾ cup pecans
- ¼ cup maple syrup
- 2 tablespoons coconut oil
- ¼ cup water
- 1 teaspoon vanilla extract
- Pinch of salt

DIRECTIONS

1. Preheat oven to 350° F and grease an 8x8" pan.
2. Combine all of the ingredients in a medium bowl and mix well until a smooth batter forms.
3. Pour the batter into the greased pan and bake for about 30 minutes, until the edges are golden brown and the center is firm.
4. If the glaze is being used, combine all the ingredients together in a blender, and process until smooth and creamy.
5. Allow to cool completely in the pan before glazing.

CUT OUT SUGAR COOKIES

Prep time: 10 minutes | Cook time: 15-20 minutes | Serves: 6

INGREDIENTS

- 1 cup raw cashews
- ½ cup coconut flour
- 1 tablespoon tapioca flour
- ¼ teaspoon salt
- ½ teaspoon baking soda
- ¼ cup coconut oil
- ½ teaspoon vanilla extract
- 1 egg
- ¼ cup honey

DIRECTIONS

1. Do not preheat your oven. The timing is based on putting the cookies into a cold oven.
2. Grind the cashews into a flour in your food processor.
3. Then add in the coconut flour, salt, baking soda and tapioca flour and pulse to combine. Add the coconut oil, vanilla, egg and honey and pulse until you have a dough.
4. Roll out the dough between two sheets of parchment and cut with cookie cutters of your choice. Place them on a piece of parchment paper and then bake at 350° F for 15-20 minutes or until golden brown on the edges. Decorate if desired.

LEMON TART

Prep time: 15 minutes | Cook time: 20-30 minutes | Serves: 8

INGREDIENTS

- Crust:
- 1 cup almond butter
- 1 cup unsweetened shredded coconut
- ⅔ cup walnuts
- 1-2 tablespoons honey
- Pinch of salt

Topping:
- 5 eggs, whisked
- ⅓ cup honey
- ⅓ cup coconut oil
- 4 lemons, juiced
- 1 cup blueberries
- ½ cup raspberries

DIRECTIONS

1. Place all crust ingredients in food processor and mix until it comes together.
2. Add crust ingredients to an 8x8" dish and press down to form an even crust. Put in refrigerator for about 20 minutes. While the crust is hardening, make the lemon filling.
3. Place a small saucepan over medium heat, then add your eggs, honey, coconut oil, and lemon juice to the saucepan and whisk together.
4. Continue stirring together until mixture begins to thicken.
5. Once the lemon mixture has thickened, remove from heat, and place in bowl to cool in the fridge for about 20 minutes.
6. When the filling is cooled, spread it over the crust then place your berries on the top and decorate as desired.

CHOCOLATE CUPCAKES

Prep time: 15 minutes | Cook time: 25-30 minutes | Serves: 6

INGREDIENTS

Cupcakes:
- ½ cup dates, pitted
- 3 eggs
- 2 egg whites
- ⅓ cup coconut oil
- ¼ cup full-fat coconut milk
- ¼ cup coconut flour
- ¼ cup cocoa powder, unsweetened
- 1 teaspoon cinnamon
- 1 teaspoon vanilla extract
- ½ teaspoon baking soda
- Pinch of salt

Frosting:
- 1 cup chocolate chips (least sugar possible)
- ¼ cup coconut oil or unsalted butter
- Pinch of salt

DIRECTIONS

1. Preheat the oven to 350°F. Add the dates to a food processor and process until the dates become a sticky ball. Add the coconut oil, coconut milk, eggs and egg whites to the processor with the dates and blend until everything is completely smooth.
2. Pour the date mixture into a large bowl and then add all the dry ingredients. Mix to incorporate. Scoop batter into a lined muffin tin and bake for 22-25 minutes or until a toothpick comes out clean when inserted in the center.
3. Place the frosting ingredients in a small bowl and gradually melt and stir until smooth, then place in the freezer for 5-10 minutes. Re-stir the frosting to soften it up. You want it to be a spreadable consistency.
4. Once the cupcakes are done baking, let them completely cool, or the icing will melt. Frost and decorate as desired.

BANANA UPSIDE DOWN CAKE

Prep time: 15 minutes | Cook time: 25-30 minutes | Serves: 8

INGREDIENTS

Fruit Layer:
- 2 tablespoons coconut oil, melted
- 1 small banana, sliced
- 2 tablespoons walnuts
- 1 teaspoon cinnamon

Cake Layer:
- 2 eggs, beaten
- ⅓ cup maple syrup
- ¼ cup coconut milk or unsweetened almond milk
- 1 teaspoon vanilla extract
- ½ teaspoon baking soda
- 1 teaspoon apple cider vinegar
- 1 small banana, mashed
- ⅓ cup coconut flour

DIRECTIONS

1. Preheat oven to 350° F, and lightly grease a 9" cake pan. Place the melted coconut oil in the bottom of the pan and swirl it to coat the bottom.
2. Sprinkle 2 tablespoons coconut sugar and 1 teaspoon cinnamon on the coconut oil, then layer the banana slices on top of the sugar and then the walnut pieces if desired. Set aside.
3. In a large mixing bowl combine all the cake layer ingredients except for the coconut flour. Mix thoroughly, then add the coconut flour and mix well, scraping down the sides of bowl. Make sure there are no clumps of coconut flour.
4. Carefully spread the batter out evenly on top of the bananas and bake for about 25 minutes or until top of cake is browned and center is set. Allow the cake to cool before taking out of the pan.

FLOURLESS CHOCOLATE CAKE

Prep time: 10 minutes | Cook time: 25-30 minutes | Serves: 8-10

INGREDIENTS

- 6 ounces dark chocolate, (least sugar possible)
- ¼ cup unsweetened applesauce
- ¼ cup melted coconut oil
- ½ cup + 2 tablespoons cocoa powder, (unsweetened)
- 2 tablespoons hot coffee
- 3 eggs
- ¾ cup honey
- Pinch of salt
- 1 teaspoon vanilla extract

* Optional for serving: Unsweetened coconut powder for dusting, fresh whipped cream, etc.

DIRECTIONS

1. Preheat oven to 350° F and grease a 9" spring-form pan.
2. In a bowl melt chocolate, then mix in coconut oil and stir until combined.
3. Add in remaining ingredients and mix completely
4. Pour mixture in pan and bake for 25 minutes, or until a toothpick comes out clean when inserted in the center.
5. Let cool completely before removing from pan and dust with additional cocoa powder or whipped cream, if desired.

COCONUT LIME POPSICLES

Prep time: 4 hours | Serves: 8

INGREDIENTS

- 3 cups coconut cream or full-fat coconut milk
- Liquid stevia, to taste
- 4 tablespoons fresh lime juice

DIRECTIONS

1. Place all ingredients in a medium sized mixing bowl. Whisk until well combined. Taste and add additional lime juice if desired.
2. Pour into popsicle molds and freeze for 4 hours or until frozen solid. To serve, run pops under warm water to loosen and serve immediately.

CHOCOLATE BANANA MILKSHAKE

Prep time: 5-10 minutes | Serves: 4

INGREDIENTS

- 12 large ice cubes
- 1 banana
- ½ teaspoon vanilla extract
- 2 tablespoons cocoa powder, unsweetened
- 1 cup + 2 tablespoons full-fat coconut milk (plus more if needed)

DIRECTIONS

1. Place all ingredients in a blender. Process until smooth and creamy. Pour into glasses and serve.

APPLE CRISP

Prep time: 15 minutes | Cook time: 45-60 minutes | Serves: 6-8

INGREDIENTS

Filling:
- 6 tart apples peeled, cored and sliced
- ¼ cup coconut sugar
- 2 tablespoons coconut flour
- 2 teaspoon cinnamon

Topping:
- 1 cup chopped walnuts
- ½ cup almond meal
- ½ cup coconut flour
- ¼ cup coconut oil
- ¼ cup coconut sugar
- 1 teaspoon cinnamon

DIRECTIONS

1. Preheat the oven to 350° F. Mix the apples with the coconut sugar, coconut flour and cinnamon, then place in an 8x8" baking dish.
2. Stir together all the ingredients for the topping and mix until incorporated but still crumbly. Crumble the topping over the apples and bake for about 45 minutes or until the top is golden brown.

STUFFED BAKED BANANAS

Prep time: 10 minutes | Cook time: 15-20 minutes | Serves: 1

INGREDIENTS

- 1 medium sized banana
- 1-2 tablespoons almond butter or nut butter of choice
- ½ teaspoon cinnamon (optional)
- ½ tablespoon dark chocolate chips (least sugar possible)
- Other toppings such as shredded coconut, chopped nuts, chopped dried fruit, etc.

DIRECTIONS

1. Preheat the oven to 375° F.
2. Leave the peel on the banana and carefully cut about ½" deep into and down the length of the banana. Do not cut through the peel on the bottom.
3. With the back of a spoon, widen the cut to make room for the almond butter and toppings.
4. Spoon the almond butter throughout the slice in the banana and sprinkle with cinnamon and other toppings.
5. Wrap completely in aluminum foil and bake for 15 minutes. Remove from oven and let cool for a few minutes or until it's cool enough to handle. Unwrap and either eat directly from the foil or transfer to a plate.

FRUIT AND NUT BARS

Prep time: 15 minutes | Serves: 8-10

INGREDIENTS

- 1 cup raw almonds
- ½ cup raw pecans
- 12 Medjool dates, pitted
- 1 cup dried cherries, no sugar added
- 2 tablespoons coconut oil
- ½ cup finely shredded coconut, no sugar added
- ¼ teaspoon salt

DIRECTIONS

1. In a food processor, pulse the nuts and the salt until finely chopped but still chunky. Some will be ground up almost like almond meal but they will not all be consistent.
2. Pour the nuts into a mixing bowl then add the dates and cherries to the food processor and process until it makes a paste.
3. Add the coconut oil to the dates and cherries and mix together.
4. Add the date mixture to the nuts and shredded coconut and mix together by hand until combined.
5. Grease a baking sheet with either unsalted butter or coconut oil and spread the bar mixture out into your desired thickness, about ½" thick.
6. Refrigerate until firm then cut into squares. Store in the refrigerator.

AMBROSIA MACAROONS

Prep time: 10 minutes | Cook time: 10-15 minutes | Serves: 12

INGREDIENTS

- 6 egg whites
- ¼ teaspoon salt
- ½ cup honey
- 1 tablespoon vanilla
- 2 teaspoon orange zest
- 3 cups unsweetened shredded coconut

DIRECTIONS

1. Preheat your oven to 350° F. In a medium sized mixing bowl, whip the egg whites and salt until stiff.
2. Fold in honey, vanilla, zest and coconut.
   Scoop the batter into the desired size onto a parchment lined baking sheet.
3. Bake at 350˚F for 10-15 minutes, until lightly browned.

My take on junk food...

All across the world, teenagers, college students and you adults survive on junk food... and when I say "junk food", I'm talking about hamburgers, pizza, chocolate chip cookies, fried chicken, and the like.

Part of the reason is because junk food is comforting.

And because it's so comforting, we don't tend to stop eating once we leave our college-age years behind.

Now, not all junk food is bad, but the way it's traditionally made and packaged, you're cutting corners with your health.

I figured out that there are ways to make your favorite snacks at home by using healthier and more-nutritious ingredients.

On the next pages, you'll find everything from dairy-free brownies that are moist and delicious to a gluten-free pizza crust that's as satisfying as what you'll find in a New York Pizza.

You don't have to give up eating the things you love the most - and that even includes pasta!

All you have to do is use recipes that have whole food like I'm going so show you in just a moment. I hope you love these as much as me!

JUNK FOODS

BURGERS

Prep Time: 15 minutes | Cook Time: 10-15 minutes | Serves: 4

INGREDIENTS

- 2 tablespoons coconut oil, divided
- ½ pound cremini mushrooms, minced
- 1½ pounds ground beef
- 1½ teaspoon salt
- Freshly ground black pepper, to taste

Optional for serving: lettuce, tomato, bacon, onions, cheese, pickles, roasted veggies, etc.

DIRECTIONS

1. Heat 1 tablespoon of the oil in a large skillet and add the mushrooms. Sauté until the liquid they released has evaporated. Mix the mushrooms into the beef and season with salt and pepper.

2. Shape into 4 even patties, about ¾" thick. Heat up the other tablespoon of oil in the large skillet and add the patties. Cook on medium heat for about 5-6 minutes, then flip and cook the other side. Take off the heat whenever the desired doneness is reached.

SPAGHETTI

Prep Time: 10 minutes | Cook Time: 6-8 hours | Serves: 4

INGREDIENTS

- 1 spaghetti squash
- 2 pounds ground beef
- 1 bunch carrots
- 1 bunch kale
- 6-8 ounces mushrooms
- 2-4 small zucchini
- 4-5 medium tomatoes
- 1 bunch mixed herbs (oregano, thyme, rosemary)
- 24 ounces strained tomatoes
- 7 ounces tomato paste
- ½ cup avocado oil
- Parmesan cheese, optional

DIRECTIONS

1. Chop all veggies, place in a blender or food processor, and blend one cup at a time. Remove the herbs from the stems and mince in a clean coffee grinder.
2. Combine all ingredients except for the spaghetti squash in the slow cooker and cook on Low for 6-8 hours. Stir occasionally.
3. Preheat oven to 400° F. Cut the spaghetti squash in half lengthwise, place cut side down on a baking sheet and bake for 30-35 minutes or until the outside of it is soft when pressed.
4. Remove the seeds and discard. Then scrape out the rest of the squash into a bowl. Serve with the sauce on top.

FRENCH TOAST

Prep Time: 10 minutes | Cook Time: 10-15 minutes | Serves: 4

INGREDIENTS

- 6-8 slices gluten free bread
- 6 eggs
- 1½ cups full-fat coconut milk
- 2 tablespoons vanilla extract
- ½ teaspoon cinnamon, optional
- Pinch of nutmeg, optional
- Pinch of salt
- 2-3 tablespoons unsalted butter
- 2-3 tablespoons coconut oil

DIRECTIONS

1. Whisk together the eggs, coconut milk, vanilla, salt and spices (if using) in a medium bowl. Place the bread in a baking dish large enough to hold the slices in a single layer. Pour the egg mixture over bread and soak for about 5 minutes. Turn the slices over and soak for another 5 minutes.

2. Melt about 1 tablespoon each coconut oil in a large skillet over medium heat. Fry half the bread slices until golden brown, about 2 to 3 minutes per side. Repeat with the remaining bread. Serve with butter and maple syrup or fresh fruit, if desired.

WAFFLES

Prep Time: 10 minutes | Cook Time: 10-15 minutes | Serves: 2-3

INGREDIENTS

- Coconut oil spray, as needed
- ½ cup almond flour
- ½ cup coconut flour
- ½ cup tapioca flour
- 2 teaspoons baking powder
- ¼ teaspoon salt
- 5 tablespoons butter, melted
- 1 pastured egg
- 1 teaspoon vanilla
- ½-1 cups coconut milk
- 1 teaspoon apple cider vinegar

DIRECTIONS

1. Heat up the waffle iron.
2. In a small bowl, mix the vinegar with the coconut milk and set aside. Combine all the dry ingredients in a large bowl and combine the egg, vanilla and melted butter in a separate bowl. Whisk the wet into the dry and stir until smooth. Stir in the coconut milk, adding more if needed to thin out the batter if it's too thick. It should be the consistency of thick pudding.
3. Grease the waffle iron with coconut spray and place a scoop or two of batter in the center of the iron. Cook until the waffle is golden brown and serve with fresh fruit, syrup or anything you like!

MACARONI AND CHEESE

Prep Time: 20 minutes | Cook Time: 60-70 minutes | Serves: 8-10

INGREDIENTS

- 1 bag rice pasta macaroni
- 3 tablespoons unsalted butter
- 1 teaspoon salt
- Dash of cayenne, optional
- Freshly ground pepper, to taste
- 2 tablespoons sorghum flour
- 1½ tablespoons tapioca starch
- 1 cup heavy cream
- 1½ cups milk
- 4 cups + 1 cup (for sprinkling) shredded cheese (cheddar, jack, Parmesan, etc.)

DIRECTIONS

1. Cook the pasta in large pot until al dente, then rinse well with cold water and set aside.
2. In the pot used to cook the pasta, melt the butter over medium heat then add the spices. Whisk in the sorghum flour and tapioca starch, then whisk in the cream and milk. Make sure there are no lumps of flour.
3. Slowly add the cheese about 1 cup at a time. Keep the heat low and constantly stir until all the cheese has melted. Turn the heat off, stir in the noodles, then pour into a large oven safe casserole dish.
4. The dish can be covered and kept in the fridge for 1-2 days or can be baked immediately. Bake with foil covering the top at 375° F for about 15 minutes then remove the foil and allow the top to crisp and lightly brown. Broiling helps speed up the process, just be sure to not burn the top!

CHOCOLATE CHIP COOKIES

Prep Time: 10 minutes | Cook Time: 10-15 minutes | Serves: 8

INGREDIENTS

- ¼ cup palm shortening
- ⅓ cup honey
- 1 egg
- 1 tablespoon vanilla extract
- 1½ cups almond flour
- 2 tablespoons coconut flour
- ½ teaspoon baking soda
- ½ teaspoon salt
- ½ cup dark chocolate chips, (least sugar possible)

DIRECTIONS

1. Preheat oven to 350° F.
2. By hand or in a food processor, cream the butter, honey, egg, and vanilla until smooth and fluffy. Add the almond flour, coconut flour, baking soda and salt and mix until everything is incorporated. Stir in the chocolate chips.
3. Scoop dough out into 1½" balls and place on a parchment lined baking sheet. Press each ball of dough down slightly until they are about ½" thick. Bake for 9-12 minutes or until slightly golden around the edges.

ICE CREAM

Prep Time: 10 minutes | Serves: 2-3

INGREDIENTS

- 2 cups milk of choice or full-fat coconut milk
- 1½ teaspoons vanilla extract
- 2 frozen bananas
- ¼ cup honey

DIRECTIONS

1. Combine all ingredients in a blender or food processor and blend until thick and smooth.
2. Serve immediately or store in an air-tight container in the freezer. Other flavors can be made by substituting other frozen fruits or extracts and any desired toppings can be used as well.

PIZZA

Prep Time: 15 minutes | Cook Time: 30-40 minutes | Serves: 2

INGREDIENTS

Gluten-free pizza crust (recipe below):

- Toppings of choice: cheese, olives, uncured pepperoni, sausage, mushrooms, sun dried tomatoes, artichoke hearts, roasted garlic, roasted red peppers, pesto, chicken, pineapple, etc.

For the crust:

- 2 cups mashed yuca, peeled and cut into large pieces
- 1 teaspoon coconut oil
- 2 heaping tablespoons unsalted butter
- 2 tablespoons coconut flour
- ½ teaspoon salt
- ½ teaspoon oregano

DIRECTIONS

1. Preheat the oven to 375° F. Boil the yuca in until fork tender, then combine all the ingredients except for coconut flour in a food processor. Puree until a dough is formed and scoop the dough onto a piece of parchment paper dusted with coconut flour. Knead in the remaining coconut flour and allow to cool.
2. Roll the dough out into a crust and bake for 15-20 minutes on a parchment lined baking sheet. Flip the dough over and let the other side cook until golden brown.
3. Spread the sauce evenly across the crust and then the toppings of your choice.
4. Bake until the edge of the crust is lightly browned and cheese is melted, about 10-15 min.

BROWNIES

Prep Time: 15 minutes | Cook Time: 40-50 minutes | Serves: 8-12

INGREDIENTS

- 1 (16 oz.) jar creamy roasted almond butter
- 2 pastured eggs
- 1¼ cups honey
- 1 tablespoon vanilla extract
- ½ cup unsweetened cocoa powder
- ½ teaspoon salt
- 1 teaspoon baking soda
- 1 cup dark chocolate chips (least sugar possible)

DIRECTIONS

1. Preheat oven to 325° F. Lightly grease a 9x13" baking dish with coconut oil and line with parchment paper.
2. In a large bowl, combine the almond butter with the eggs, honey and vanilla until smooth
3. Stir in the cocoa powder, salt and baking soda, then fold in the chocolate chips. Pour the batter in the prepared pan and bake for 35-40 minutes or until a toothpick comes out clean when inserted in the center.

PEANUT BUTTER CUPS

INGREDIENTS

For the peanut butter:
- 1 cup peanut butter, smooth or crunchy
- ¼ cup honey
- ¼ cup coconut oil, melted

For the chocolate:
- ½ cup dark chocolate chips, melted (least sugar possible)
- ¼ cup coconut oil, melted

DIRECTIONS

1. Line a standard muffin tin. Combine the peanut butter, honey and melted coconut oil and fill each muffin tin about half way. There should be enough for 8-9. Place in the freezer to harden.
2. For the chocolate layer, combine the melted chocolate chips and coconut oil and whisk until combined. Pour over the peanut butter layer and return to the freezer until hardened.

CHEESECAKE

Prep Time: 15 minutes | Cook Time: 60-70 minutes | Serves: 8

INGREDIENTS

Crust:
- ½ cup almonds
- ½ cup pecans
- ½ cup unsweetened coconut flakes
- ½ cup Medjool dates
- 2 tablespoons coconut oil, melted

Cheesecake:
- 8 ounces cream cheese
- 16 ounces full-fat Greek yogurt
- 4 eggs
- ¾ cup honey
- 1 teaspoon vanilla extract
- ½ lemon, juiced and zested
- ½ teaspoon salt

DIRECTIONS

1. Blend dates in a food processor until they become a smooth paste. Remove and add the nuts. Pulse until they are a coarse meal. Add to the dates and stir in the coconut oil. Mix until well incorporated, then press evenly into the bottom of a 8" spring-form pan.

2. Combine the cheesecake ingredients in a large mixing bowl, blending eggs into the batter one at a time. Use a hand mixer to blend until smooth. Pour the batter onto the crust and bake for about an hour. The center should be puffed and no longer jiggly. Chill before serving.

FRIED CHICKEN

Prep Time: 20 minutes | Cook Time: 50-60 minutes | Serves: 6

INGREDIENTS

- 4 eggs
- ¼ cup full-fat coconut milk
- 3 tablespoons coconut oil, melted (plus more for cooking)
- ¼ cup coconut flour
- ¼ teaspoon baking powder
- ¼ teaspoon salt

DIRECTIONS

1. In a large bowl, whisk the eggs, coconut milk and coconut oil until combined. In another bowl, whisk together the coconut flour, baking powder and salt.
2. Add the dry ingredients to the wet and mix until there no lumps.
3. Grease a large skillet with coconut oil and place over medium heat. Pour batter into the pan and allow to cook about 3 to 4 minutes. Once bubbles start to form, flip and cook on the other side about 1 to 2 minutes.
4. Serve with your favorite toppings.

JALAPEÑO POPPERS

Prep Time: 15 minutes | Cook Time: 20-30 minutes | Serves: 4

INGREDIENTS

- 12 jalapeños
- 4 ounces cream cheese, softened
- 8 ounces uncured bacon, cut in half
- Salt and freshly ground pepper, to taste
- 1 tablespoon avocado oil

DIRECTIONS

1. Preheat the oven to 350° F. Toss the jalapeños in avocado oil and sprinkle with salt and pepper. Roast for 10 minutes. Cut down the center of one side of the jalapeño (do not cut off the top or cut completely open) and remove the seeds.
2. Turn the temperature up to 450° F. Fill each one with cream cheese and shape back into the shape of the jalapeño.
3. Wrap with 1 piece of bacon and secure with a toothpick if necessary. Bake on a parchment lined sheet pan until the bacon is crisp for 15-20 minutes.

DONUTS

Prep Time: 15 minutes | Cook Time: 10-15 minutes | Serves: 6-8

INGREDIENTS

Donuts:
- ½ cup unsalted butter, softened
- ¾ cup coconut sugar
- 2 eggs
- 2 teaspoons vanilla
- 2⅔ cups all-purpose gluten-free flour
- 1½ teaspoons baking powder
- ¼ teaspoon baking soda
- ¾ teaspoon salt
- 1 cup full-fat coconut milk

For dusting:
- 4 tablespoons salted butter, melted
- ½ cup coconut sugar
- 1½ tablespoons cinnamon

DIRECTIONS

1. Preheat oven to 425° F. Spray a donut pan with non-stick cooking spray.
2. In a bowl, cream together the butter and coconut sugar until smooth. Add the eggs and vanilla, and whisk until smooth. In another bowl, whisk together the flour mix, baking powder, baking soda and salt.
3. Alternate adding the flour mixture and the milk to the butter mixture, beginning and ending with the flour. Mix until everything is incorporated.
4. Pipe the batter into the pan and bake for about 8-10 minutes or until they are golden brown and a toothpick comes out clean when inserted in the center. Remove from the oven and let cool. Repeat with remaining batter and spray the pan between batches.
5. Combine the cinnamon with the coconut sugar. Brush each donut with the melted butter, then dip in the cinnamon-sugar mixture to coat.

PANCAKES

Prep Time: 10 minutes | Cook Time: 10-15 minutes | Serves: 2

INGREDIENTS

- ¼ cup coconut flour
- 4 eggs
- ¼ cup milk
- 3 tablespoons coconut oil, melted (plus more for cooking)
- ¼ teaspoon baking powder
- ¼ teaspoon salt

DIRECTIONS

1. In a large bowl, whisk the eggs, milk and coconut oil until combined. In another bowl, whisk together the coconut flour, baking powder and salt.
2. Add the dry ingredients to the wet and mix until there no lumps.
   Grease a large skillet with coconut oil and place over medium heat.
3. Pour batter into the pan and allow to cook about 3 to 4 minutes. Once bubbles start to form, flip and cook on the other side about 1 to 2 minutes.
4. Serve with your favorite toppings.

FETTUCCINE ALFREDO

Prep Time: 15 minutes | Cook Time: 40-50 minutes | Serves: 4

INGREDIENTS

- 1 spaghetti squash, cooked
- 1 pound chicken breast, boneless and skinless
- 1 shallot, minced
- 4 cloves garlic, minced
- 4 tablespoons salted butter
- 1 teaspoon freshly ground pepper
- ½ teaspoon salt
- 2 cups heavy cream
- 6 white mushrooms, sliced
- 2 cups broccoli, steamed
- 1 cup Parmesan cheese, shredded

DIRECTIONS

1. Preheat the oven to 375° F and lightly grease a baking sheet. Place the spaghetti squash cut side down and roast until soft, about 35-45 minutes. Scrape out the strands once cooled.
2. In a large skillet over medium heat, melt the butter, then add the shallots. Sauté for a few minutes then add the garlic and sauté for another few minutes. Add the cream, salt and pepper and reduce the heat to low and simmer for about 20 minutes.
3. Season the chicken with salt and pepper and cook as desired (grill, saute, bake, etc.). Slice into strips and set aside.
4. Add the mushrooms to the sauce and simmer for about 10-15 minutes.
5. Increase the heat to medium and add the spaghetti squash and gently mix it all around. Add the cheese, chicken and broccoli and stir until the cheese is melted and incorporated into the sauce.

CINNAMON ROLLS

Prep Time: 20 minutes | Cook Time: 15-20 minutes | Serves: 4-6

INGREDIENTS

For the dough:
- 1 cup milk, warmed
- 1 standard packet quick-rise yeast
- 2½ cups gluten-free all purpose flour (plus more for kneading, if necessary)
- ½ cup coconut sugar
- 1½ teaspoons baking powder
- ¼ teaspoon baking soda
- ½ teaspoon salt
- ¼ cup unsalted butter, very cold and cubed into small pieces

For the filling:
- ¼ cup unsalted butter, melted
- ½-⅔ cup coconut sugar
- 1-2 tablespoon cinnamon

For the icing:
- 1 ounce cream cheese, softened
- 2 tablespoons unsalted butter, softened
- 1 teaspoon vanilla extract
- Coconut sugar, to taste

DIRECTIONS

1. Stir the yeast into the warm milk with a pinch of coconut sugar and allow it to sit for 5-10 minutes. In a large bowl, combine all the dry ingredients. Using a food processor or by hand, cut the cold butter into the dry ingredients until it forms pea sized pieces.

2. Slowly pour the warmed milk into the dry ingredients and mix just until the dough just comes together, then lay it out on a lightly floured surface. Roll the dough out into a rectangle, about ¼" thick. If the dough is too sticky, knead in a little more flour (about 1 tablespoon at a time) until it's kneadable but not overly sticky and then proceed to roll out.

3. Evenly spread the melted butter over the dough and sprinkle with coconut sugar and cinnamon. Roll the dough up tightly, cut into pieces about 2" long and place in a lightly greased baking dish. Preheat the oven to 400° F and place the pan of rolls on top of the oven to rise slightly while it preheats. Bake for about 15 minutes or until golden brown.

4. Stir the icing ingredients together until smooth. Drizzle the over the warm rolls before serving. Enjoy!

NUTRITION FACTS INDEX

Page 10

Gluten-Free Banana Loaf

Servings per container 12
Serving size   1/12 of entire recipe

Amount per serving
Calories   133
*grams of Macronutrient

Total Fat	7g
Total Carbohydrates	15g
Protein	4g

* The grams of each macronutrient are approximate to the ingredient quantities used in each recipe. Calories may vary slightly depending on the brand used.

Page 12

Gingerbread Loaf

Servings per container 12
Serving size   1/12 of entire recipe

Amount per serving
Calories   161
*grams of Macronutrient

Total Fat	10g
Total Carbohydrates	17g
Protein	3g

* The grams of each macronutrient are approximate to the ingredient quantities used in each recipe. Calories may vary slightly depending on the brand used.

Page 14

Raspberry Lemon Poppyseed

Servings per container 12
Serving size   1/12 of entire recipe

Amount per serving
Calories   257
*grams of Macronutrient

Total Fat	16g
Total Carbohydrates	25g
Protein	5g

* The grams of each macronutrient are approximate to the ingredient quantities used in each recipe. Calories may vary slightly depending on the brand used.

Page 16

Gluten-Free Chocolate Zucchini Bread

Servings per container 12
Serving size   1/12 of entire recipe

Amount per serving
Calories   138
*grams of Macronutrient

Total Fat	10g
Total Carbohydrates	11g
Protein	4g

* The grams of each macronutrient are approximate to the ingredient quantities used in each recipe. Calories may vary slightly depending on the brand used.

Page 18

Gluten-Free Bread

Servings per container 12
Serving size   1/12 of entire recipe

Amount per serving
Calories   175
*grams of Macronutrient

Total Fat	15g
Total Carbohydrates	6g
Protein	6g

* The grams of each macronutrient are approximate to the ingredient quantities used in each recipe. Calories may vary slightly depending on the brand used.

Page 20

Gluten-Free Buttermilk Loaf

Servings per container 12
Serving size   1/12 of entire recipe

Amount per serving
Calories   342
*grams of Macronutrient

Total Fat	27g
Total Carbohydrates	23g
Protein	7g

* The grams of each macronutrient are approximate to the ingredient quantities used in each recipe. Calories may vary slightly depending on the brand used.

Page 22

Gluten-Free Cherry Almond Bread

Servings per container 12
Serving size   1/12 of entire recipe

Amount per serving
Calories   401
*grams of Macronutrient

Total Fat	28g
Total Carbohydrates	31g
Protein	10g

* The grams of each macronutrient are approximate to the ingredient quantities used in each recipe. Calories may vary slightly depending on the brand used.

Page 24

Gluten-Free Cranberry Orange Bread

Servings per container 12
Serving size   1/12 of entire recipe

Amount per serving
Calories   183
*grams of Macronutrient

Total Fat	12g
Total Carbohydrates	17g
Protein	4g

* The grams of each macronutrient are approximate to the ingredient quantities used in each recipe. Calories may vary slightly depending on the brand used.

Page 26

Gluten-Free Carrot Bread

Servings per container 12
Serving size   1/12 of entire recipe

Amount per serving
Calories   277

*grams of Macronutrient

Total Fat	16g
Total Carbohydrates	32g
Protein	4g

* The grams of each macronutrient are approximate to the ingredient quantities used in each recipe. Calories may vary slightly depending on the brand used.

Page 28

Gluten-Free Zucchini Bread

Servings per container 12
Serving size   1/12 of entire recipe

Amount per serving
Calories   187

*grams of Macronutrient

Total Fat	13g
Total Carbohydrates	15g
Protein	5g

* The grams of each macronutrient are approximate to the ingredient quantities used in each recipe. Calories may vary slightly depending on the brand used.

Page 29

Gluten -Free "Cornbread"

Servings per container 6
Serving size   1/6 of entire recipe

Amount per serving
Calories   152

*grams of Macronutrient

Total Fat	15g
Total Carbohydrates	11g
Protein	6g

* The grams of each macronutrient are approximate to the ingredient quantities used in each recipe. Calories may vary slightly depending on the brand used.

Page 30

Cinnamon Apple Bread

Servings per container 12
Serving size   1/12 of entire recipe

Amount per serving
Calories   369

*grams of Macronutrient

Total Fat	29g
Total Carbohydrates	20g
Protein	11g

* The grams of each macronutrient are approximate to the ingredient quantities used in each recipe. Calories may vary slightly depending on the brand used.

Page 34

Spiked Lemonade

Servings per container 1
Serving size   1 Drink

Amount per serving
Calories   121

*grams of Macronutrient

Total Fat	0g
Total Carbohydrates	5g
Protein	1g

* The grams of each macronutrient are approximate to the ingredient quantities used in each recipe. Calories may vary slightly depending on the brand used.

Page 34

Grapefruit Mojito

Servings per container 1
Serving size   1 Drink

Amount per serving
Calories   154

*grams of Macronutrient

Total Fat	0g
Total Carbohydrates	12g
Protein	1g

* The grams of each macronutrient are approximate to the ingredient quantities used in each recipe. Calories may vary slightly depending on the brand used.

Page 36

Moscow Mule

Servings per container 1
Serving size   1 Drink

Amount per serving
Calories   146

*grams of Macronutrient

Total Fat	0g
Total Carbohydrates	3g
Protein	0g

* The grams of each macronutrient are approximate to the ingredient quantities used in each recipe. Calories may vary slightly depending on the brand used.

Page 36

Coconut Coolers

Servings per container 1
Serving size   1 Drink

Amount per serving
Calories   169

*grams of Macronutrient

Total Fat	0g
Total Carbohydrates	8g
Protein	1g

* The grams of each macronutrient are approximate to the ingredient quantities used in each recipe. Calories may vary slightly depending on the brand used.

Page 37

Fruit Explosion

Servings per container 1
Serving size   1 Drink

Amount per serving
Calories   212

*grams of Macronutrient

Total Fat	0g
Total Carbohydrates	39g
Protein	4g

* The grams of each macronutrient are approximate to the ingredient quantities used in each recipe. Calories may vary slightly depending on the brand used.

Page 40

NorCal Margarita

Servings per container 1
Serving size   1 Drink

Amount per serving
Calories   206

*grams of Macronutrient

Total Fat	0g
Total Carbohydrates	19g
Protein	2g

* The grams of each macronutrient are approximate to the ingredient quantities used in each recipe. Calories may vary slightly depending on the brand used.

Page 42

Mojito

Servings per container 1
Serving size   1 Drink

Amount per serving
Calories   114

*grams of Macronutrient

Total Fat	0g
Total Carbohydrates	4g
Protein	2g

* The grams of each macronutrient are approximate to the ingredient quantities used in each recipe. Calories may vary slightly depending on the brand used.

Page 44

Piña Colada

Servings per container 1
Serving size   1 Drink

Amount per serving
Calories   288

*grams of Macronutrient

Total Fat	12g
Total Carbohydrates	46g
Protein	1g

* The grams of each macronutrient are approximate to the ingredient quantities used in each recipe. Calories may vary slightly depending on the brand used.

Page 46

Cucumber Lime Cooler

Servings per container 1
Serving size   1 Drink

Amount per serving
Calories   126

*grams of Macronutrient

Total Fat	0g
Total Carbohydrates	9g
Protein	1g

* The grams of each macronutrient are approximate to the ingredient quantities used in each recipe. Calories may vary slightly depending on the brand used.

Page 47

Watermelon Mojito

Servings per container 1
Serving size   1 Drink

Amount per serving
Calories   154

*grams of Macronutrient

Total Fat	0g
Total Carbohydrates	26g
Protein	2g

* The grams of each macronutrient are approximate to the ingredient quantities used in each recipe. Calories may vary slightly depending on the brand used.

Page 47

Pineapple Drop

Servings per container 1
Serving size   1 Drink

Amount per serving
Calories   181

*grams of Macronutrient

Total Fat	0g
Total Carbohydrates	50g
Protein	1g

* The grams of each macronutrient are approximate to the ingredient quantities used in each recipe. Calories may vary slightly depending on the brand used.

Page 48

Katie Cosmo

Servings per container 1
Serving size   1 Drink

Amount per serving
Calories   168

*grams of Macronutrient

Total Fat	0g
Total Carbohydrates	45g
Protein	0g

* The grams of each macronutrient are approximate to the ingredient quantities used in each recipe. Calories may vary slightly depending on the brand used.

Page 48

Kombucha Margarita

Servings per container 2
Serving size   1/2 of entire recipe

Amount per serving
Calories   171

*grams of Macronutrient

Total Fat	0g
Total Carbohydrates	30g
Protein	2g

* The grams of each macronutrient are approximate to the ingredient quantities used in each recipe. Calories may vary slightly depending on the brand used.

Page 50

Blackberry Mint Mojito

Servings per container 1
Serving size   1 Drink

Amount per serving
Calories   127

*grams of Macronutrient

Total Fat	0g
Total Carbohydrates	34g
Protein	0g

* The grams of each macronutrient are approximate to the ingredient quantities used in each recipe. Calories may vary slightly depending on the brand used.

Page 51

Blueberry Bliss

Servings per container 1
Serving size   1 Drink

Amount per serving
Calories   156

*grams of Macronutrient

Total Fat	0g
Total Carbohydrates	26g
Protein	1g

* The grams of each macronutrient are approximate to the ingredient quantities used in each recipe. Calories may vary slightly depending on the brand used.

Page 51

Strawberry Peach Paradise

Servings per container 1
Serving size   1 Drink

Amount per serving
Calories   160

*grams of Macronutrient

Total Fat	0g
Total Carbohydrates	41g
Protein	2g

* The grams of each macronutrient are approximate to the ingredient quantities used in each recipe. Calories may vary slightly depending on the brand used.

Page 52

Kombucha Margarita

Servings per container 2
Serving size   1/2 of entire recipe

Amount per serving
Calories   171

*grams of Macronutrient

Total Fat	0g
Total Carbohydrates	30g
Protein	2g

* The grams of each macronutrient are approximate to the ingredient quantities used in each recipe. Calories may vary slightly depending on the brand used.

Page 52

Raspberry Citrus Sparkler

Servings per container 1
Serving size   1 Drink

Amount per serving
Calories   188

*grams of Macronutrient

Total Fat	0g
Total Carbohydrates	51g
Protein	1g

* The grams of each macronutrient are approximate to the ingredient quantities used in each recipe. Calories may vary slightly depending on the brand used.

Page 53

Paradise Mint Fusion

Servings per container 1
Serving size   1 Drink

Amount per serving
Calories   183

*grams of Macronutrient

Total Fat	0g
Total Carbohydrates	34g
Protein	2g

* The grams of each macronutrient are approximate to the ingredient quantities used in each recipe. Calories may vary slightly depending on the brand used.

Page 53

Strawberry Mojito

Servings per container 1
Serving size   1 Drink

Amount per serving
Calories   144

*grams of Macronutrient

Total Fat	0g
Total Carbohydrates	23g
Protein	2g

* The grams of each macronutrient are approximate to the ingredient quantities used in each recipe. Calories may vary slightly depending on the brand used.

Page 56

Sweetened Whipped Cream with Fresh Strawberries

Servings per container 4
Serving size 1/4 of entire recipe

Amount per serving
Calories 170

*grams of Macronutritent

Total Fat	12g
Total Carbohydrates	15g
Protein	2g

* The grams of each macronutrient are approximate to the ingredient quantities used in each recipe. Calories may vary slightly depending on the brand used.

Page 58

Chocolate Dipped Banana Bites

Servings per container 4
Serving size 1/4 of entire recipe

Amount per serving
Calories 338

*grams of Macronutritent

Total Fat	19g
Total Carbohydrates	43g
Protein	6g

* The grams of each macronutrient are approximate to the ingredient quantities used in each recipe. Calories may vary slightly depending on the brand used.

Page 60

Cinnamon Almonds with Berry Compote

Servings per container 2
Serving size 1/2 of entire recipe

Amount per serving
Calories 171

*grams of Macronutritent

Total Fat	8g
Total Carbohydrates	25g
Protein	3g

* The grams of each macronutrient are approximate to the ingredient quantities used in each recipe. Calories may vary slightly depending on the brand used.

Page 62

Vanilla Chia Pudding

Servings per container 4
Serving size 1/4 of entire recipe

Amount per serving
Calories 559

*grams of Macronutritent

Total Fat	31g
Total Carbohydrates	68g
Protein	14g

* The grams of each macronutrient are approximate to the ingredient quantities used in each recipe. Calories may vary slightly depending on the brand used.

Page 64

Key Lime Pie

Servings per container 12
Serving size 1/12 of entire recipe

Amount per serving
Calories 267

*grams of Macronutritent

Total Fat	19g
Total Carbohydrates	23g
Protein	4g

* The grams of each macronutrient are approximate to the ingredient quantities used in each recipe. Calories may vary slightly depending on the brand used.

Page 66

Almond Butter Brownies

Servings per container 12
Serving size 1/12 of entire recipe

Amount per serving
Calories 431

*grams of Macronutritent

Total Fat	29g
Total Carbohydrates	40g
Protein	9g

* The grams of each macronutrient are approximate to the ingredient quantities used in each recipe. Calories may vary slightly depending on the brand used.

Page 68

Chocolate Chip Cookies

Servings per container 8
Serving size 1/8 of entire recipe

Amount per serving
Calories 304

*grams of Macronutritent

Total Fat	23g
Total Carbohydrates	25g
Protein	6g

* The grams of each macronutrient are approximate to the ingredient quantities used in each recipe. Calories may vary slightly depending on the brand used.

Page 70

Fruit Crisp

Servings per container 6
Serving size 1/6 of entire recipe

Amount per serving
Calories 420

*grams of Macronutritent

Total Fat	33g
Total Carbohydrates	33g
Protein	6g

* The grams of each macronutrient are approximate to the ingredient quantities used in each recipe. Calories may vary slightly depending on the brand used.

Page 71

Vanilla Coconut Ice Cream

Servings per container 3
Serving size 1/3 of entire recipe

Amount per serving
Calories 476

*grams of Macronutritent

Total Fat	32g
Total Carbohydrates	47g
Protein	1g

* The grams of each macronutrient are approximate to the ingredient quantities used in each recipe. Calories may vary slightly depending on the brand used.

Page 72

Chocolate Mousse

Servings per container 2
Serving size 1/2 of entire recipe

Amount per serving
Calories 226

*grams of Macronutritent

Total Fat	20g
Total Carbohydrates	12g
Protein	3g

* The grams of each macronutrient are approximate to the ingredient quantities used in each recipe. Calories may vary slightly depending on the brand used.

Page 73

Snickerdoodles

Servings per container 8
Serving size 1/8 of entire recipe

Amount per serving
Calories 290

*grams of Macronutritent

Total Fat	21g
Total Carbohydrates	25g
Protein	7g

* The grams of each macronutrient are approximate to the ingredient quantities used in each recipe. Calories may vary slightly depending on the brand used.

Page 74

Almond Butter Blondies

Servings per container 8
Serving size 1/8 of entire recipe

Amount per serving
Calories 333

*grams of Macronutritent

Total Fat	22g
Total Carbohydrates	33g
Protein	7g

* The grams of each macronutrient are approximate to the ingredient quantities used in each recipe. Calories may vary slightly depending on the brand used.

Page 76

Fruit and Nut Clusters

Servings per container 12
Serving size 1/12 of entire recipe

Amount per serving
Calories 321

*grams of Macronutritent

Total Fat	22g
Total Carbohydrates	35g
Protein	1g

* The grams of each macronutrient are approximate to the ingredient quantities used in each recipe. Calories may vary slightly depending on the brand used.

Page 77

No Bake Peanut Butter Pie

Servings per container 12
Serving size 1/12 of entire recipe

Amount per serving
Calories 412

*grams of Macronutritent

Total Fat	35g
Total Carbohydrates	24g
Protein	9g

* The grams of each macronutrient are approximate to the ingredient quantities used in each recipe. Calories may vary slightly depending on the brand used.

Page 78

Raspberry Almond Bars

Servings per container 8
Serving size 1/8 of entire recipe

Amount per serving
Calories 431

*grams of Macronutritent

Total Fat	32g
Total Carbohydrates	33g
Protein	10g

* The grams of each macronutrient are approximate to the ingredient quantities used in each recipe. Calories may vary slightly depending on the brand used.

Page 80

Pumpkin Bars

Servings per container 12
Serving size 1/12 of entire recipe

Amount per serving
Calories 202

*grams of Macronutritent

Total Fat	14g
Total Carbohydrates	16g
Protein	4g

* The grams of each macronutrient are approximate to the ingredient quantities used in each recipe. Calories may vary slightly depending on the brand used.

Page 81

Cut Out Sugar Cookies

Servings per container 6
Serving size 1/6 of entire recipe

Amount per serving
Calories 306

*grams of Macronutritent

Total Fat	22g
Total Carbohydrates	28g
Protein	6g

* The grams of each macronutrient are approximate to the ingredient quantities used in each recipe. Calories may vary slightly depending on the brand used.

Page 82

Lemon Tart

Servings per container 12
Serving size 1/12 of entire recipe

Amount per serving
Calories 363

*grams of Macronutritent

Total Fat	28g
Total Carbohydrates	24g
Protein	9g

* The grams of each macronutrient are approximate to the ingredient quantities used in each recipe. Calories may vary slightly depending on the brand used.

Page 84

Chocolate Cupcakes

Servings per container 6
Serving size 1/6 of entire recipe

Amount per serving
Calories 564

*grams of Macronutritent

Total Fat	37g
Total Carbohydrates	59g
Protein	6g

* The grams of each macronutrient are approximate to the ingredient quantities used in each recipe. Calories may vary slightly depending on the brand used.

Page 85

Banana Upside Down Cake

Servings per container 8
Serving size 1/8 of entire recipe

Amount per serving
Calories 173

*grams of Macronutritent

Total Fat	10g
Total Carbohydrates	20g
Protein	3g

* The grams of each macronutrient are approximate to the ingredient quantities used in each recipe. Calories may vary slightly depending on the brand used.

Page 86

Flourless Chocolate Cake

Servings per container 10
Serving size 1/10 of entire recipe

Amount per serving
Calories 248

*grams of Macronutritent

Total Fat	13g
Total Carbohydrates	34g
Protein	4g

* The grams of each macronutrient are approximate to the ingredient quantities used in each recipe. Calories may vary slightly depending on the brand used.

Page 87

Coconut Lime Popsicles

Servings per container 8
Serving size 1/8 of entire recipe

Amount per serving
Calories 182

*grams of Macronutritent

Total Fat	18g
Total Carbohydrates	4g
Protein	0g

* The grams of each macronutrient are approximate to the ingredient quantities used in each recipe. Calories may vary slightly depending on the brand used.

Page 88

Chocolate Banana Milkshake

Servings per container 2
Serving size 1/2 of entire recipe

Amount per serving
Calories 313

*grams of Macronutritent

Total Fat	25g
Total Carbohydrates	23g
Protein	2g

* The grams of each macronutrient are approximate to the ingredient quantities used in each recipe. Calories may vary slightly depending on the brand used.

Page 90

Apple Crisp

Servings per container 6
Serving size 1/6 of entire recipe

Amount per serving
Calories 482

*grams of Macronutritent

Total Fat	30g
Total Carbohydrates	56g
Protein	8g

* The grams of each macronutrient are approximate to the ingredient quantities used in each recipe. Calories may vary slightly depending on the brand used.

Page 91

Stuffed Baked Bananas

Servings per container 1
Serving size   **Entire recipe**

Amount per serving
Calories   381

*grams of Macronutrient

Total Fat	21g
Total Carbohydrates	47g
Protein	9g

* The grams of each macronutrient are approximate to the ingredient quantities used in each recipe. Calories may vary slightly depending on the brand used.

Page 92

Fruit and Nut Bars

Servings per container 12
Serving size   1/12 of entire recipe

Amount per serving
Calories   245

*grams of Macronutrient

Total Fat	14g
Total Carbohydrates	31g
Protein	4g

* The grams of each macronutrient are approximate to the ingredient quantities used in each recipe. Calories may vary slightly depending on the brand used.

Page 94

Ambrosia Macaroons

Servings per container 12
Serving size   1/12 of entire recipe

Amount per serving
Calories   151

*grams of Macronutrient

Total Fat	10g
Total Carbohydrates	16g
Protein	3g

* The grams of each macronutrient are approximate to the ingredient quantities used in each recipe. Calories may vary slightly depending on the brand used.

Page 98

Burgers

Servings per container 4
Serving size   1/4 of entire recipe

Amount per serving
Calories   372

*grams of Macronutrient

Total Fat	25g
Total Carbohydrates	2g
Protein	36g

* The grams of each macronutrient are approximate to the ingredient quantities used in each recipe. Calories may vary slightly depending on the brand used.

Page 100

Spaghetti

Servings per container 8
Serving size   1/8 of entire recipe

Amount per serving
Calories   480

*grams of Macronutrient

Total Fat	27g
Total Carbohydrates	31g
Protein	29g

* The grams of each macronutrient are approximate to the ingredient quantities used in each recipe. Calories may vary slightly depending on the brand used.

Page 101

Waffles

Servings per container 4
Serving size   1/4 of entire recipe

Amount per serving
Calories   605

*grams of Macronutrient

Total Fat	37g
Total Carbohydrates	59g
Protein	7g

* The grams of each macronutrient are approximate to the ingredient quantities used in each recipe. Calories may vary slightly depending on the brand used.

Page 102

Mac and Cheese

Servings per container 10
Serving size   1/10 of entire recipe

Amount per serving
Calories   520

*grams of Macronutrient

Total Fat	33g
Total Carbohydrates	40g
Protein	19g

* The grams of each macronutrient are approximate to the ingredient quantities used in each recipe. Calories may vary slightly depending on the brand used.

Page 106

Chocolate Chip Cookies

Servings per container 8
Serving size   1/8 of entire recipe

Amount per serving
Calories   304

*grams of Macronutrient

Total Fat	23g
Total Carbohydrates	25g
Protein	6g

* The grams of each macronutrient are approximate to the ingredient quantities used in each recipe. Calories may vary slightly depending on the brand used.

Page 108

Ice Cream

Servings per container 3
Serving size   1/3 of entire recipe

Amount per serving
Calories   476

*grams of Macronutrient

Total Fat	32g
Total Carbohydrates	47g
Protein	1g

* The grams of each macronutrient are approximate to the ingredient quantities used in each recipe. Calories may vary slightly depending on the brand used.

Page 110

Brownies

Servings per container 12
Serving size   1/12 of entire recipe

Amount per serving
Calories   445

*grams of Macronutrient

Total Fat	29g
Total Carbohydrates	50g
Protein	10g

* The grams of each macronutrient are approximate to the ingredient quantities used in each recipe. Calories may vary slightly depending on the brand used.

Page 112

Peanut Butter Cups

Servings per container 12
Serving size   1/12 of entire recipe

Amount per serving
Calories   282

*grams of Macronutrient

Total Fat	23g
Total Carbohydrates	17g
Protein	5g

* The grams of each macronutrient are approximate to the ingredient quantities used in each recipe. Calories may vary slightly depending on the brand used.

Page 114

Cheesecake

Servings per container 8
Serving size   1/8 of entire recipe

Amount per serving
Calories   505

*grams of Macronutritent

Total Fat	30g
Total Carbohydrates	52g
Protein	13g

* The grams of each macronutrient are approximate to the ingredient quantities used in each recipe. Calories may vary slightly depending on the brand used.

Page 115

Fried Chicken

Servings per container 6
Serving size   1/6 of entire recipe

Amount per serving
Calories   902

*grams of Macronutritent

Total Fat	63g
Total Carbohydrates	17g
Protein	71g

* The grams of each macronutrient are approximate to the ingredient quantities used in each recipe. Calories may vary slightly depending on the brand used.

Page 116

Jalapeño Poppers

Servings per container 4
Serving size   1/4 of entire recipe

Amount per serving
Calories   394

*grams of Macronutritent

Total Fat	36g
Total Carbohydrates	4g
Protein	18g

* The grams of each macronutrient are approximate to the ingredient quantities used in each recipe. Calories may vary slightly depending on the brand used.

Page 118

Donuts

Servings per container 8
Serving size   1/8 of entire recipe

Amount per serving
Calories   473

*grams of Macronutritent

Total Fat	25g
Total Carbohydrates	60g
Protein	6g

* The grams of each macronutrient are approximate to the ingredient quantities used in each recipe. Calories may vary slightly depending on the brand used.

Page 119

Pancakes

Servings per container 2
Serving size   1/2 of entire recipe

Amount per serving
Calories   448

*grams of Macronutritent

Total Fat	40g
Total Carbohydrates	10g
Protein	15g

* The grams of each macronutrient are approximate to the ingredient quantities used in each recipe. Calories may vary slightly depending on the brand used.

Page 120

Fettuccine Alfredo

Servings per container 8
Serving size   1/8 of entire recipe

Amount per serving
Calories   599

*grams of Macronutritent

Total Fat	47g
Total Carbohydrates	21g
Protein	32g

* The grams of each macronutrient are approximate to the ingredient quantities used in each recipe. Calories may vary slightly depending on the brand used.

Page 121

Cinnamon Rolls

Servings per container 6
Serving size   1/6 of entire recipe

Amount per serving
Calories   559

*grams of Macronutritent

Total Fat	28g
Total Carbohydrates	76g
Protein	8g

* The grams of each macronutrient are approximate to the ingredient quantities used in each recipe. Calories may vary slightly depending on the brand used.